KEEP UP THE GOOD WORK, CHARLIE BROWN

Selected Cartoons from SPEAK SOFTLY AND CARRY A BEAGLE, Vol. III

Charles M. Schulz

CORONET BOOKS
Hodder Fawcett, London

First published in the United States
of America by Fawcett Crest Books

Coronet edition 1980

Printed in Great Britain for Hodder
Fawcett Ltd., Mill Road, Dunton Green,
Sevenoaks, Kent (Editorial Office: 47
Bedford Square, London, WC1 3DP) by
C. Nicholls & Company Ltd
The Philips Park Press, Manchester

ISBN 0 340 24875 0

Keep up the good work, Charlie Brown!

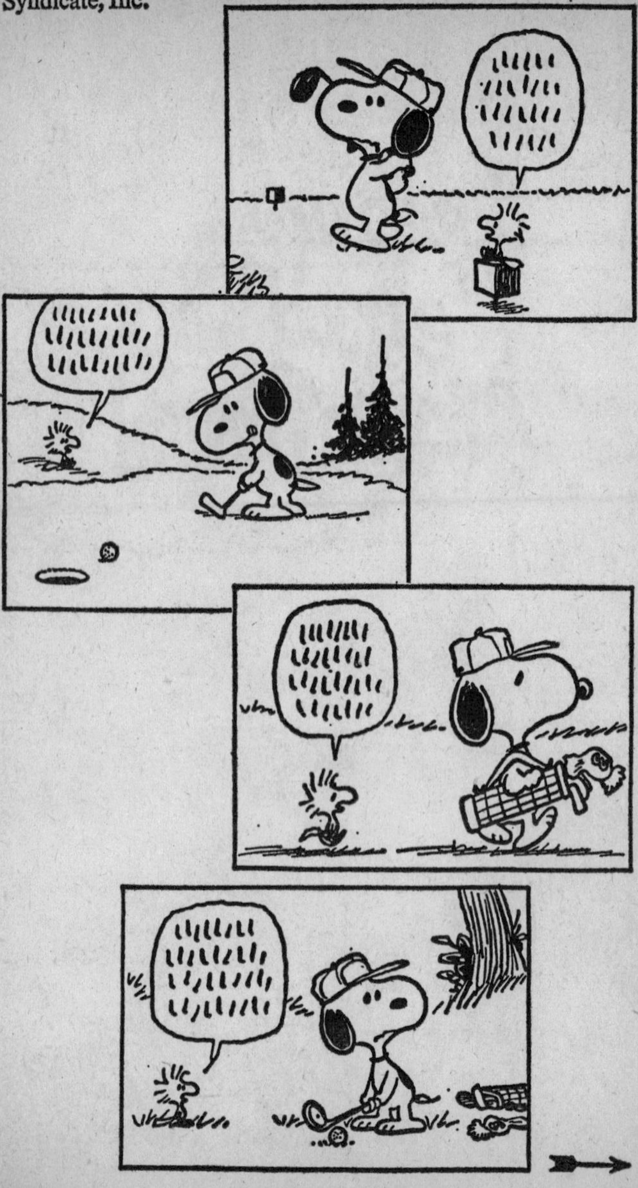

YOUR STOMACH? OKAY, COME ON IN... I'LL CALL THE VET..

YES, SIR...I'M SORRY TO WAKE YOU UP...

HE SAID YOU SHOULD GO OUT AND EAT SOME GRASS...

HE SAID THAT'S WHAT THE AVERAGE DOG DOES INSTINCTIVELY WHEN HIS STOMACH IS UPSET...

WET GRASS AT TWO O'CLOCK IN THE MORNING?!?

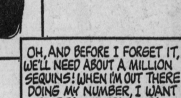

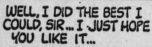

IT'S NO USE, SIR...I CAN'T FIX YOUR HAIR!

MAYBE I SHOULD GO OVER TO SEE CHUCK'S DAD...HE'S A BARBER, AND SEEING AS HOW I'M CHUCK'S FRIEND, MAYBE HE'LL GIVE ME A DISCOUNT...

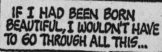

IF I HAD BEEN BORN BEAUTIFUL, I WOULDN'T HAVE TO GO THROUGH ALL THIS...

ALL MY LIFE I'VE DREAMED OF LOOKING LIKE PEGGY FLEMING...INSTEAD, I LOOK LIKE BABE RUTH!

Schulz

Once there were two mice who lived in a museum.

One evening after the museum had closed, the first mouse crawled into a huge suit of armor.

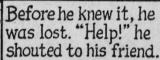

Before he knew it, he was lost. "Help!" he shouted to his friend.

"Help me make it through the knight!"

POOR WOODSTOCK DOESN'T KNOW HOW TO TAKE CARE OF HIMSELF IN EMERGENCIES...

HE'S PROBABLY SNOWED UNDER, OF FROZEN STIFF, OR...

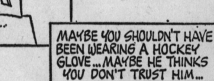

The Gift

It was the holiday season.

She and her husband had decided to attend a performance of King Lear.

It was their first night out together in months.

During the second act one of the performers became ill.

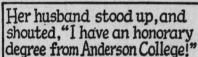

The manager of the theater walked onto the stage, and asked, "Is there a doctor in the house?"

Her husband stood up, and shouted, "I have an honorary degree from Anderson College!"

It was at that moment when she decided not to get him anything for Christmas.

SCHULZ

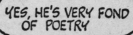

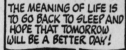

NOW, HERE IS MY EXCLUSIVE...IT USED TO BE THOUGHT THAT ROCK SNAKES WERE DANGEROUS, BUT MY AUTHORITY SAYS THIS IS NOT SO...

A ROCK SNAKE CANNOT THROW VERY HIGH, YOU SEE, SO THEREFORE, ALL HE CAN DO IS HIT YOU ON THE BACK OF THE LEG...SO SAYS MY AUTHORITY!

MA'AM?

LINUS VAN PELT.... YES, MA'AM..

SHE SAID SHE REMEMBERS YOU FROM WHEN YOU WERE IN HER CLASS!

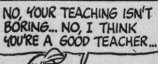

YES, MA'AM..I WAS TOLD TO REPORT TO THE PRINCIPAL...

WELL, I'VE BEEN FALLING ASLEEP IN CLASS, I GUESS, AND MY TEACHER'S KIND OF UPSET ABOUT IT..

THE PRINCIPAL IS BUSY? THAT'S OKAY...I CAN WAIT...

Z

I REALLY APPRECIATE YOUR COMING OVER TO STAY WITH ME, SNOOPY...

MY DAD WILL BE WORKING LATE FOR ANOTHER WEEK, AND I SURE GET SCARED BEING IN THE HOUSE ALONE..

C'MON, I'LL SHOW YOU OUR GUEST ROOM...YOU'LL HAVE IT ALL TO YOURSELF...

AND I HOPE YOU'LL LIKE THE WATERBED...

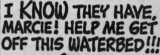

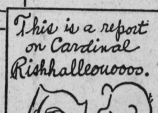

This is a story of Greed.

I'M GLAD TO SEE YOU'RE WRITING ABOUT GREED...

ONE OF THE SECRETS OF GOOD WRITING IS TO DEAL WITH REAL HUMAN EMOTIONS

Joe Greed was born in a small town in Colorado.

"I DREAMED THAT MY MOTHER HAD COME BACK TO THE NEST AND THAT SHE AND I WERE FLYING THROUGH THE AIR TOGETHER, AND I WAS SO HAPPY..."

"THEN I WOKE UP... MY NEST WAS SITTING ON A FENCE POST... MY MOTHER REALLY HADN'T COME HOME... I WAS ALL ALONE! *SIGH*"

SNIF

I THINK I'LL GIVE UP PRACTICAL JOKES...

Allegretto

I NOTE THAT YOU DIDN'T SEND ME A VALENTINE THIS YEAR...

I HAVE THE FEELING THAT IT WAS NOT AN OVERSIGHT...I HAVE THE FEELING THAT IT WAS DELIBERATE!

HOWEVER....